NORTH-EAST ENGLAND *from the air*

DAVID GODDARD
Text by
MELVYN JONES

MYRIAD
LONDON

First published in 2009 by Myriad Books Limited
35 Bishopsthorpe Road, London SE26 4PA

ISBN 1 84746 268 5
EAN 978 1 84746 268 8

Designed by Jerry Goldie Graphic Design
Printed in China

www.myriadbooks.com

CONTENTS

INTRODUCTION

North-East England contains some of the most dramatic and beautiful landscapes in Britain. They include an extraordinary range of physical landscapes and a bewildering variety of human landscapes. And these are made even more impressive when seen from the air.

Inland the landscape ranges from the high, rounded, heather, cotton grass and bracken-covered hills of the Cheviots in the Northumberland National Park, to the valleys of upper Teesside. There is a varied and spectacular coastline – from the long, sandy, often almost deserted beaches of Northumberland and North Yorkshire to the vertical cliff coastlines of Marsden Cliffs and Blackhall Rocks and the magnificent North Yorkshire coast from Saltburn to Robin Hood's Bay. Both the Farne Islands just a short boat ride from Seahouses and the island of Lindisfarne located at the end of a causeway have dramatic settings and are full of historical and wildlife interest. Linking the high moorlands and the coast in large parts of the region is a tranquil agricultural landscape dotted with small villages and market towns reached by quiet country roads.

The human landscape of North-East England is full of contrasts. The fact that we are in Border country is very evident in the landscape. Some of the most exciting landmarks are military, such as the remains of the mighty Hadrian's Wall and its forts at Housesteads and Chesters and the medieval castles of Alnwick, Bamburgh, Dunstanburgh, Warkworth, Prudhoe, Durham and Raby. In complete contrast are the remains of the medieval religious houses at Lindisfarne, Hulne, Egglestone, Finchale, Guisborough and Whitby that form spectacular reminders of a bygone age. The region is also full of interesting small and medium-sized towns such as Berwick, Alnwick, Corbridge and Hexham in Northumberland, Bishop Auckland in County Durham, Yarm on Teesside, Whitby in North Yorkshire and, most interesting of all set on its crag in a meander of the river Wear, the city of Durham.

The large metropolitan areas of Tyneside, Wearside and Teesside are full of architectural gems such as Grey Street in Newcastle, the grid-iron central streets of the Victorian "new town" of Middlesbrough and the modern architecture of the Gateshead Sage or the Winter Gardens in Sunderland. And for the connoisseur of bridges there can be no better place than the North-East. There are three bridges over the Tweed in Berwick, a spectacular series of bridges over the Tyne between Newcastle and Gateshead, the Transporter Bridge and the Newport Bridge across the Tees, the 43-arch railway viaduct at Yarm, the railway-turned-road bridge at Bishop Auckland and the 18th century bridge across the river South Tyne at Hexham – the list is almost endless.

Just turn the page and begin your virtual flight across this fascinating region...

Melvyn Jones

left: Housesteads Fort is one of the best preserved of the 16 forts associated with Hadrian's Wall.

Northumberland

England's most northerly county is a county of superlatives. It has arguably the best and quietest beaches in the country. It has some of the best-preserved small historic towns such as Berwick, Alnwick and Morpeth. The Northumberland National Park is the most tranquil wilderness area in England and even the modern human-made landscape features like Kielder Water and Kielder Forest fit into the landscape seamlessly. Being in Border country some of its most exciting landmarks are military such as the remains of the mighty Hadrian's Wall and its forts and the medieval castles at Alnwick, Bamburgh, Dunstanburgh and Warkworth. And for wildlife enthusiasts there are the wild white cattle of Chillingham and the seabird and grey seal colonies of the Farne Islands. What more can anyone wish for?

Castle Country

Everywhere the visitor turns in Northumberland there seems to be a castle on the horizon. There are the Roman forts associated with Hadrian's Wall (right), the medieval castles of Dunstanburgh and Bamburgh (far right) by the coast, Alnwick (above) in a market town, Warkworth looming over a village and Chillingham isolated inland. Moreover there is the romantic Edwardian Lindisfarne Castle re-built from a 16th century fort and reached across a causeway only at low tide, and Victorian Cragside that is not quite a castle but ought to be with its castle-like name and site high above Debdon Burn.

Berwick-upon-Tweed

This small traditional market town (its population in 2001 was 11,685), the most northerly town in England, stands at the mouth of the river Tweed. In medieval times in Border wars and skirmishes it changed hands between the Scots and the English 13 times before finally becoming part of England in 1482. It was made a free burgh in 1551 in an agreement between Edward VI and Mary Queen of Scots. Elizabeth I, afraid of an attack from joint French and Scottish forces, fortified the town by building stone walls around it, designed to withstand attack from artillery. They survive to this day and are clearly seen above. The fortifications became redundant in 1606 when England and Scotland were united under James VI of Scotland who became James I of England. The links between England and Scotland go further than transport links. The town's football club, Berwick Rangers, play in the Scottish Football League.

Berwick has always been an important gateway between Scotland and England and this has meant bridging the river Tweed. In the foreground above is the 15-span stonebuilt Berwick Bridge constructed between 1611 and 1634 to replace the old wooden bridge; beyond that is the Royal Tweed Bridge of 1928 built to carry the A1 (the Great North Road) and in the background is the 28-arch Royal Border Railway Bridge built by Robert Stephenson and opened by Queen Victoria in 1850.

BERWICK AT WAR

The town retained its free burgh status until 1885 when it officially became part of England. The free burgh status confers on Berwick an odd accolade according to one apocryphal story. When this country declared war on Russia at the outbreak of the Crimean War in 1853, it is said that the declaration was in the name of Great Britain, Ireland and Berwick-upon-Tweed. But when the war ended, the peace treaty omitted the name of Berwick-upon-Tweed and so, if the story is true, the town would still be, in strict legal terms, at war with Russia. To end hostilities, the mayor of Berwick signed a peace treaty with a Soviet official in 1966!

LINDISFARNE

Lindisfarne or Holy Island is a magnet for all visitors to Northumberland. It is one mile (1.5km) off the coast and is accessible by vehicle or on foot by a three-mile long causeway (far right) at low tide only. The causeway is closed for two hours before high tide and for three hours afterwards. There is so much to see on Lindisfarne: the ruins of the 12th century Benedictine priory, the romantic Lindisfarne Castle and the Lindisfarne Centre with its interactive exhibition about the Lindisfarne Gospels. And for nature lovers there are interesting wildflowers and an ever-changing birdlife. On the sand dunes that cover the northern part of the island the wildflowers include some of Arctic origin and rare orchids. The island is also a landfall for birds on their spring and autumn migrations including a variety of geese, ducks and waders and occasionally the rare northern gull.

Lindisfarne Priory

St Aidan, who came from Iona, the centre of Christianity in Scotland, founded the first monastery here in the Anglo-Saxon period and later St Cuthbert lived and died here. The beautiful illuminated Lindisfarne Gospels, now in the British Library, were compiled here. Viking raids in 793 partially destroyed the first monastery. For safekeeping, St Cuthbert's remains were taken to the mainland during the Viking incursions and they survive in Durham Cathedral. The monastery was re-built as a Benedictine priory in the 12th century and dissolved by Henry VIII in 1537. Some of the stone from the priory was used to build a 16th century fort on a dramatic rocky outcrop to hold a garrison of troops to protect the harbour. The surviving upstanding ruins are a reminder to the modern visitor of how isolated and cut off from the rest of humanity these early monastic communities were.

LINDISFARNE CASTLE

The fort, by then in a state of dereliction, was bought in 1902 by Edward Hudson, the editor of *Country Life*, with a view to converting it into a holiday home. For this work he employed Sir Edwin Lutyens, the most famous English architect of the first half of the 20th century. The result is a sympathetic conversion with small rooms full of intimate decoration and cosy furnishings. The castle came into the ownership of the National Trust in 1944. From the windows and viewing terraces the view in one direction is over the harbour towards the mainland (left) and in the opposite direction over a walled paddock that leads to a small walled garden (below and top right). The garden was designed by the great garden designer Gertrude Jekyll, as a mixed vegetable and ornamental garden. It has now been restored by the National Trust as a flower garden.

BAMBURGH CASTLE

Dominating the coastal landscape between Holy Island to the north and Dunstanburgh to the south is the impressive Bamburgh Castle, once the home of the kings of Northumbria, built on a rocky outcrop 150ft (46m) high. Lord Armstrong, the Victorian inventor, innovator and engineer, began the restoration of Bamburgh Castle in the 1890s. The central keep was built by the Normans and it was in a state of dereliction before Armstrong began its restoration. It is still the home of the Armstrong family. On the seaward side of the castle are 20ft (6m) high sand dunes which lead to an extensive sandy beach with views to Lindisfarne Castle and the Farne Islands.

Farne Islands

The Farne Islands are chiefly treeless naked rocks, between 15 and 28 in number depending on the state of the tide. They contain important colonies of seabirds. Longstone Island (above) is home to 3,800 grey seals, one of the most important colonies in Europe of this rare species. Longstone Island has the Longstone lighthouse (right) famous because of its association with Grace Darling, the daughter of the lighthouse-keeper. In September 1838 the steamship *Forfarshire*, sailing from Hull to Dundee with 39 passengers and 24 members of crew on board, experienced boiler trouble and struck the rocks in tremendous seas and gale force winds. Grace, then aged 22, and her father launched a rowing boat and after two journeys in the howling gale they rescued nine passengers. She became a national heroine but died only four years later.

Inner Farne (left) is home to appproximately 1,000 breeding Arctic terns, almost 3,000 guillemots, about 100 razorbills and 13,000 breeding pairs of puffins. Also on Inner Farne is St Cuthbert's chapel, supposed to be the site of St Cuthbert's cell of AD676. Restored in the 19th century on the instructions of the Archdeacon of Durham, it has a stained-glass window and a memorial to Grace Darling.

Beadnell

The panoramic view above looks northwards along the coast with Beadnell in the foreground and Seahouses in the background. Beadnell (bottom left) has changed its role over time. The old limekilns by the harbour indicate that lime-burning was once important as was herring fishing. Now it is a popular holiday resort with visitors drawn by its long curving beach and its handy location on Northumberland's beautiful, historic coastline. But a few fishermen still ply their trade using the small traditional east coast fishing boat called a *coble*, with its high prow and stern, used for fishing up to 15 miles off the coast.

Seahouses

Seahouses (right) was established as an offshoot of North Sunderland, with which it has long since merged, as a base for fishermen. It is still a small fishing port, but also doubles as a coastal resort and, above all, as the starting point for boat excursions to the Farne Islands.

Craster

The name Craster is derived from *crawe-cestre*, an old fortification inhabited by crows. The village (above) was once famous for its quarried stone that was shipped to London to be made into kerbstones. The stone, from a quarry just inland of the village that was closed in the 1930s, was whinstone, a hard, dark basaltic rock. The round, stone base at the end of the harbour is the remains of a tower that was the terminus of an aerial ropeway that brought the stone from the quarry. Although still a fishing village, Craster was once a flourishing fishing port, with nearly two dozen boats supplying herrings to be made into kippers in its smokehouses. Now its huddle of houses around the harbour, that was constructed in 1906, makes an attractive start for the many thousands of visitors beginning their coastal walk towards Dunstanburgh Castle.

Dunstanburgh Castle

Dunstanburgh Castle is now owned by the National Trust and managed by English Heritage. The ruins stand on a basalt crag more than 100ft (30m) high. The castle was built by Thomas, Earl of Lancaster, in the early 14th century. The castle was protected on two sides by sheer cliffs and the sea. The highest and most imposing part of the ruin is the large gatehouse in the form of two D-shaped towers on either side of an arched entrance. At the end of the 14th century the castle came into the hands of John of Gaunt who made many alterations including converting the gatehouse into a keep. Running away on either side of the keep are the curtain walls. Located above the sea cliff on the western curtain wall is the Lilburn Tower which was used as a watchtower. The ruins are said to be haunted by Sir Guy the Seeker, a knight who failed to wake a princess who had been put under a spell. When the wind howls round the castle, the noise is said to be Sir Guy moaning and groaning in despair.

The ruined castle can only be approached on foot, from Craster to the south and Embleton to the north, with the romantic ruins silhouetted against the skyline in the distance throughout most of the walk. The walk to the castle along the footpath from Craster just above the shoreline is as compelling as the ruinous castle itself. The visitor can drop from the footpath down towards the rocky shore and just sit on the rocks and watch the waves crashing onshore or try to identify the seabirds. In some quiet pool in summer there may be a female eider with her chicks while further out at sea, shags, in ones or twos can often be seen flying fast and low just above the water. And in late autumn or winter the visitor may be lucky and see migrant snow buntings.

CHEVIOT HILLS

Approached from the east along quiet gorse-lined country roads with views of farmland, moorland, and well-wooded valleys, the Cheviot Hills stretch for 35 miles (55km) from Kielder Water in the south-west to the town of Wooler in the north-east. They straddle the English-Scottish border and are crossed by only one road, the A68. Made up of broad, rounded hills, the highest point is The Cheviot at 2674ft (815m). Rock outcrops are not very frequent as the hills are covered by glacial debris and peat and the valleys by alluvial deposits. The highest summits are covered by blanket bog but the rolling lower hills and foothills are covered by acidic grassland, heather and bracken and are the home of the white Cheviot sheep.

Rothbury

The small, quiet community of Rothbury is referred to as the "Capital of Coquetdale". Sometimes described as a village and sometimes as a town, it was granted a market charter by Edward I in the 13th century. At various times it belonged to the Crown and the powerful Percy family. The bridge in Rothbury over the Coquet dates from the 15th century, a fourth arch being added to the original three-arch bridge in the 18th century. The town lies close to Cragside and its market cross was erected in 1902 as a mark of respect for Lord and Lady Armstrong of Cragside. The town is surrounded by an attractive rural landscape of moorland, hill farms and well-wooded valleys, popular with sightseers and walkers alike.

Cragside

Cragside was built between 1869 and 1884 by Lord Armstrong. The exterior is solid and imposing in its spectacular location. The interior is typically Victorian with William Morris wallpaper and William de Morgan-type tiles along the corridors. The house is full of paintings, ornaments, furniture and gadgets and was the first house in the world to be lit by hydro-electricity. And it also had a lift, telephone, and central heating long before most other private dwellings. Immediately outside the house is the Rock Garden, constructed on a steep bank heaped with rocks of every shape and size, crossed with pathways of huge slabs of stone and planted with heathers, conifers, azaleas and rhododendrons. Beyond the Rock Garden across an elegant steel bridge is the Pinetum, full of North American conifers.

Alnmouth

Alnmouth (above and below) is a small resort at the mouth of the Aln. In 1748 during its heyday as a busy port it was visited by the founder of Methodism, John Wesley. He declared the place to be wicked. Whether wicked or not, it certainly proved to be an unlucky place in which to live during the next 60 or so years. In 1778 it was attacked by cannon-fire from a ship commanded by John Paul Jones, sea captain and supporter of the rebellious American colonies and in 1806 a great storm changed the course of the river Aln and caused the silting of the harbour and its subsequent decline as a port.

Alnwick and Alnwick Castle

Alnwick is an attractive small market town with market days on Thursday and Saturday. The panoramic view above carries the eye through the town along Bodgate (Within and Without) and Narrowgate. Towering over the town is Alnwick Castle, sometimes known as the "Windsor of the North" because of its supposed similarity to Windsor Castle when seen from a distance. The castle dates back to the 11th century but was much restored in the 18th and 19th centuries. Since the early 14th century it has been the home of the Percy family, made the earls of Northumberland in 1377 and the dukes of Northumberland in 1750. Between the castle and the town a new public garden, the Alnwick Garden, was created over a number of years from 2000. It was the inspiration of the Duchess of Northumberland and designed by Jacques Wirtz and his son Peter. The centrepiece of the garden is a dramatic cascade. Sinuous stone walls swoop down the slope with paths and serpentine tunnels of hornbeam on each side. Every minute thousands of gallons of water tumble down a series of weirs and periodically jets of water, controlled by computer, shoot into the air.

Chillingham Castle

This battlemented medieval castle and stately home open to the public (above and left) was the scene of preparations for the successful attack in 1298 on William Wallace. Long galleries were added in the Elizabethan period, the surrounding parkland was landscaped by Capability Brown, and the Italianate garden was designed by Sir Jeffry Wyatville, best known for his work at Windsor Castle. In the park is a herd of wild white cattle, the sole survivors of the wild cattle that once roamed Britain. The animals are rarer than the giant panda. Free from human interference for more than 700 years, the herd stands at 80 strong.

Howick Hall

Situated only one mile from the coast, Howick Hall (right), an 18th century mansion, was the home of the earls Grey until the death of the 5th earl in 1963, when it passed to his eldest daughter and then to his grandson, the present Lord Howick of Glendale. The 2nd Earl Grey was prime minister from 1830 until 1834. The large informally planned garden is reckoned to be one of the finest coastal gardens in Britain. Among its highlights are a terraced garden, mixed borders and an exquisite woodland garden. There are also woodland walks towards the coast. A new arboretum opened in 2006.

HULNE PRIORY

Hulne Priory (below) is set in a walled park, Hulne Park, covering several thousand acres, just over two miles north-west of the centre of Alnwick. The priory was founded in the 13th century by the Carmelites or "White Friars". The Carmelites were an order of monks and nuns that originated in Palestine in the 12th century and came to Western Europe when Palestine was conquered by the Muslims. The Carmelite rule originally required adherents to live frugally and in strict isolation from the outside world. This ruling was later relaxed in order that they could care for the sick. They were a mendicant order that lived entirely on alms. The ruins of the priory include a boundary wall, a reflection of the unruly frontier country in which the priory was located in the medieval period. In the 15th century a small square pele tower was also built for protection against raiding forays from the north.

Amble and Coquet Island

The small coastal town of Amble (below) stands at the mouth of the river Coquet. It developed as a coal exporting port from the Northumberland Coalfield in the 1840s, a role which lasted until the end of the 1960s. It is now a fishing port and small holiday resort with a busy yacht marina. The tiny Coquet Island (right) lies just offshore and is now an RSPB bird reserve with large numbers of puffins, eider ducks and terns including a few roseate terns. The island had a monastery that was established as early as the 7th century. The lighthouse was built in 1841 and Grace Darling's brother was the lighthouse-keeper there.

WARKWORTH

Warkworth is an attractive stonebuilt village within a meander of the river Coquet. At one end of the village stands the majestic Warkworth Castle with its enormous 15th century keep. At the other end of the village is St Lawrence's parish church with its largely Norman chancel and tower of c1200. In the nave is a stone effigy of a knight of c1320 holding his heart in his hands.

Newbiggin

Newbiggin, or to give it its full name Newbiggin-by-the-Sea, was formerly an important grain exporting port, fishing port and coalmining village. Now all that has gone except for a few fishermen who ply their trade from *cobles*, the high-bowed open fishing boat that is still used in small numbers along the North Sea coast from Northumberland down to the Humber estuary in Yorkshire. The town was the location of a major communications breakthrough, when in 1868 the first telegraph cable from Scandinavia was pulled ashore from the North Sea. A more recent project has been the restoration and protection of the town's rapidly eroding beach. This has entailed the transportation from the Lincolnshire coast of hundreds of thousands of tons of sand and the building of a new breakwater to protect the beach. At the end of the breakwater, as shown in close-up left, is a lifelike brass statue by Sean Henry called "Couple".

ASHINGTON

Just inland of Newbiggin-by-the-Sea is a former mining town, Ashington. The town began to emerge beside the river Wansbeck in the 1840s built by the Duke of Portland who laid out streets of terraced houses to accommodate mining families who were flocking into the Northumberland coalfield. After years of prosperity based on mining employment no local colliery remains. Ashington Colliery, that began production in 1867, closed in 1988. The history of the local coalmining industry is displayed in Woodborn Mining Museum. The town is fondly remembered as the birthplace of three of the North-East's great professional footballers – Jackie Milburn ("Wor Jackie") and Jack and Sir Bobby Charlton. The photograph above shows the town, looking east to west along the Wansbeck valley.

Morpeth

Morpeth (population 14,000 in 2001) lies at an important bridging point on the river Wansbeck six miles (9.5km) from the coast and 14 miles (22km) north of Newcastle. It is the county town of Northumberland. It received its market charter as early as 1199 and before the railways came it was an important cattle market. John Leland, writing in 1540, was of the opinion that Morpeth was "a far fairer town than Alnwick". Among important buildings surviving in the town are the remains of a medieval castle, a town hall designed by Sir John Vanburgh and a 14th century church. The town is vulnerable to flooding in periods of unusual rainfall and in September 2008 it suffered its worst flood for many years when an estimated 1,000 properties were affected.

BLYTH

Blyth (left) lies on the south Northumberland coast south of the river Blyth about 13 miles (21km) north-east of Newcastle. Its origins as a port lie in the early medieval period but it was the growth of coalmining that transformed it into a busy coal exporting port and shipbuilding centre. At the height of its economic development as a port millions of tons of coal were exported every year. The prosperity of the town as a shipbuilding and repair centre can be gauged by the fact that in the first half of the 20th century there were five dry docks and four slipways for building and launching ships. The Royal Navy's first aircraft carrier, HMS *Ark Royal* was built here in 1914. These industries have now both gone but Blyth is still a busy small port. The quayside has been partly converted into a recreational space. Unusual features of the quayside are the nine wind turbines on the east pier of the Blyth Harbour Wind Farm constructed in 1992.

SEATON SLUICE

Seaton Sluice (above), made up of the merged villages of Seaton Sluice and Hartley, lies just north of the boundary between Northumberland and North Tyneside. It gets its name from the harbour work of Sir Ralph Delaval in the late 17th century. The harbour was prone to heavy silting and Sir Ralph built a walled harbour with sluice gates that were closed after the high tide had filled the harbour and thus raised the water levels behind the gates. At low tide the gates were opened and the impounded water rushed out and swept the silt away.

Northumberland National Park

Created in 1956, the Northumberland National Park, the most northerly national park in England, stretches from south of Hadrian's Wall to the Scottish border and covers more than 1,000km² – more than a quarter of the area of Northumberland. Consisting of the rounded Cheviot Hills rising to 2681ft (815m), high sandstone ridges, moorland in parts covered by blanket bog, but much of it now forested, it stretches southwestwards from the Cheviots, and through the spectacular craggy country along Hadrian's Wall. The landscape is soaked in history – Border history – stretching from the prehistoric period onwards. The scenery is magnificent, with breathtaking views of pastoral farmland, well-wooded valleys and peat moors and high crags. Wildlife is very varied. Roe deer and feral goats roam the landscape, in the woods there are pied flycatcher and redstart and on the moors curlew, dunlin, golden plover and short-eared owl. The national park is one of the least populated areas in England and so tranquillity is another of its attractive characteristics. There is something for every outdoor enthusiast whether sightseer, walker, cyclist or wildlife enthusiast.

Kielder Water

Located in the Northumberland National Park, Kielder Water (above) is the largest artificial lake by capacity in the United Kingdom – only Rutland Water has a larger surface area. It was constructed between 1975 and 1981 and opened by the Queen in 1982. After the dam was constructed it took two years for the reservoir to fill up completely. Kielder Water supplies water to the large urban areas of Tyneside, Wearside and Teesside. When first constructed it was thought by critics to be an unnecessary and costly luxury and an intrusion into a beautiful historic landscape but today, with climate change, Kielder Water is much better regarded. It has also become an important tourist destination. It is surrounded by the Kielder Forest, has visitor centres and a waterside park.

Bellingham

The village of Bellingham (above) is situated in the beautiful North Tyne valley (left) on the edge of the Northumberland National Park 18 miles (29km) north-west of Hexham and just 8 miles (13km) east of Kielder Water. It is a favourite staging post for walkers because it lies on the long-distance footpath, the Pennine Way, Britain's oldest long-distance footpath. The Pennine Way opened in 1965, and runs from Edale below Kinder Scout in the Peak District to Kirk Yetholm, just inside Scotland, a distance of 250 miles (400km).

CHIPCHASE CASTLE

The stately Chipchase Castle lies in the North Tyne valley between Bellingham to the north and Hexham to the south. It began life as a 14th century 4-storey battlemented tower house or pele tower built to provide defence against cross-Border marauders (known as *reivers*). It was converted in 1621 into a Jacobean manor house by a descendant of the medieval owner who had built the original tower. Further alterations took place in the 18th century. The house is still privately owned but the castle and its gardens are open to the public in June each year. The walled garden (seen behind the castle in the photograph on the bottom left) is now a nursery specialising in unusual hardy plants.

Hexham

The small market town of Hexham (population 11,000) lies in the valley of the South Tyne river, about 3 miles (5km) south of Hadrian's Wall and 19 miles (30km) west of Newcastle Upon Tyne. The town lies to the south of the river and is approached from the north by a multiple-arched late 18th century stone bridge (below, centre). The skyline of the town is dominated by the church (below), previously the church of Hexham Abbey. An abbey was established in 674 by Wilfrid, Bishop of York, but this was raided and pillaged by Danish invaders in 876. A second abbey, of the Augustinian order, was founded in 1114 and survived until the Dissolution of the Monasteries in the 16th century. A particularly fascinating architectural feature in the church is the barrel-vaulted crypt, assumed to be a survival from the Saxon monastery, which incorporates into its structure Roman masonry, presumably robbed from a nearby Roman fort.

Hadrian's Wall

Hadrian's Wall, named after the Roman emperor Hadrian (who ruled from AD117-138), stretched for 73 miles (117km) from Bowness on the Solway Firth in Cumbria to Wallsend near the North Sea coast. Hadrian came to Britain in person to assess the military situation in the north where constant raiding from the Caledonian tribes was a major problem. He conceived the idea of replacing the line of forts that were strung out over 72 miles between the Solway and the Tyne, and between which the enemy could pass and re-pass with relative ease, by a continuous stone wall. The wall was completed over a six year period between AD122 and AD128.

Hadrian's Wall seems to leap across the landscape. William Camden, writing in 1586, described it as running "over the high pitches and steep descents of hilles, wonderfully rising and falling". The wall was originally 15ft (4.5m) high and 8ft wide. It had a core made of rubble and mortar and each side was faced with ashlar blocks. During its construction, the masons (who were soldiers) had to be protected from attack. The wall was furnished with small forts (now known as milecastles) every Roman mile (about 1,620 yards) to accommodate the Roman soldiers on duty and between one fortlet and the next were two signalling turrets. To the north of the wall was a wide, deep ditch except in those places where the wall was built on the edge of a steep scarp like the Whin Sill (left and above). It was not meant to be a fighting platform, it was intended rather to be an elevated viewpoint for military observers. At the first sign of trouble Roman soldiers would emerge from the milecastles and signalling turrets to fight the enemy on open ground with their spears and swords. The wall was finally abandoned by the Romans in about AD400. It is now a World Heritage Site.

Housesteads Roman Fort

Housesteads, located on the edge of Whin Sill, known to the Romans as *Vercovicium*, is one of the best preserved of the 16 forts associated with Hadrian's Wall. It has the typical plan of a Roman fort. It is in the form of a walled rectangle with rounded corners. At each corner and at intervals along the walls were watchtowers. Beyond the walls was a deep ditch. In each wall there was a gate (*porta*). At the centre of the fort was the headquarters building, the *principia*, which included the cross-hall in which the commander would address his troops, together with administrative offices and a strong room. Beside the headquarters building was the commanding officer's house. Elsewhere within the fort would be barracks laid out in a tight grid-iron pattern of streets, workshops, cookhouses, a hospital and granaries. At Housesteads, the pillars on which the granaries stood to ensure good ventilation and safety from rats, have survived.

Roman forts housed either cavalry units or foot-soldiers. The fort at Housesteads, located in the moorlands and surrounded by steep, craggy slopes, would have proved difficult for mounted soldiers, and therefore was garrisoned by foot-soldiers. Whether cavalry or foot-soldiers, the garrisons of the forts along Hadrian's Wall were drawn from all parts of the Roman Empire. Although by the end of Roman rule in Britain, the Roman army contained many native-born soldiers, it is known that Roman troops stationed on Hadrian's Wall came from such places as Asturias (Spain), Batavia (Holland), Dalmatia (Croatia) and Tungria (Belgium).

HAYDON BRIDGE

The village of Haydon Bridge lies astride the river South Tyne just a few miles south of Hadrian's Wall. As its name suggests it is at a bridging point over the river, with an old stone arched bridge and beside it a modern bridge carrying the A69 between Carlisle and Newcastle Upon Tyne.

LANGLEY CASTLE

Set in a 10 acre wooded estate, Langley Castle was built as a tower house in the middle of the 14th century by the Lucy family. The degree of Border unrest at that time can be gauged by its design and structure. The central tower is guarded by four battlemented towers that are set at each corner and the stone walls are 7ft (2m) thick. The castle was a ruined shell for centuries until it was restored by the Northumberland antiquarian, Cadwallader Bates, in the late 19th century. Bates died in 1902 but Langley Castle was lived in by his widow until her death in 1932. For a time it was the premises of a school. It has now been converted into a hotel.

Chesters

Chesters House has the distinction of having within its grounds three different visitor attractions: a Roman fort, a museum of finds from the fort and a walled garden. Chesters Walled Garden, covering two acres, was for more than two centuries the vegetable and fruit garden to the house designed to provide produce 365 days a year. It has now been converted into a herb and herbaceous garden. It contains one of the largest collections of herbs in the country including the National Collections of thyme and marjoram. The thyme grows on a 30-metre raised bank, the Thyme Bank. A Roman garden grows culinary and medicinal herbs that the Romans grew in Britain. There are also long herbaceous borders and a medieval knot garden. There are red squirrels in the surrounding woodland.

CILURNUM

Chesters Roman fort, the Roman *Cilurnum*, is the best preserved fort on Hadrian's Wall designed for cavalry troops. The line of Hadrian's Wall ran through the fort and down to the North Tyne. The fort was completely covered by Nathaniel Clayton, the owner of Chesters House, in the early 19th century as part of a park landscaping scheme, but was uncovered by his son, John. The fort is now managed and maintained by English Heritage. Like Housesteads, it is a walled rectangle with rounded corners. Visible remains include the headquarters building, the commandant's house and barracks. Outside the fort towards the river North Tyne is the fort's well-preserved bath house. Originally an aqueduct brought water from the river Tyne to the bath house. The museum, built in 1896, contains important finds from the site.

Corbridge

Corbridge (right and below) with its 17th century bridge derives its name from the Roman settlement of *Corstopitum* which predates Hadrian's Wall by more than 40 years. Originally just a fort, it eventually grew into the most northerly town in the Roman Empire. The Roman site (left) is open to the public and has a small museum. Running down the middle of the site in the photograph is the Roman road that became known as Stanegate (stone street). On the right of Stanegate are the sites of the commandant's house and headquarters building, in front of the museum are the remains of the granaries and to the left of Stanegate are the remains of workshops, barracks and a temple.

PRUDHOE CASTLE

The town of Prudhoe has a population of more than 11,000 and is the largest settlement in Tynedale. The ruined Prudhoe Castle that we see today (right) dates from the 12th century and was built by the d'Umfravilles who became local lords following the Norman Conquest of 1066. It is believed that originally there was a motte and bailey castle on the site surrounded by a timber palisade. The timber palisade was replaced by a stone curtain wall with a gatehouse and then a stone keep. The walls of the keep are 10ft (3m) thick. The castle withstood at least two sieges by a Scottish army in the 12th century. The castle became the property of the Crown in 1966 and is managed by English Heritage.

BYWELL HALL

Bywell Hall (below) is located on the north bank of the Tyne 13 miles (21km) west of Newcastle Upon Tyne. The house and its surrounding estate are privately owned by the 4th Viscount Redesdale. Beautifully situated in a parkland setting in the loop of a meander on the river it was designed by James Paine and built about 1760. Some alterations were made in the 19th century.

Tyne and Wear

Tyne and Wear became a metropolitan county in 1974, but the County Council ceased to exist in 1986, and its constituent metropolitan boroughs – Newcastle Upon Tyne, Gateshead, North Tyneside, South Tyneside and Sunderland became self-governing. Some county-wide services are still run including the museums and archive service and most notably the transport authority that runs the Tyne and Wear Metro. Now a vibrant and confident place in which to live and to visit, with three large universities, the list of places to explore and enjoy is almost endless, including the Angel of the North sculpture, the bridges across the river Tyne, the Theatre Royal in Newcastle, the Sage in Gateshead, St Mary's Island and Marsden Rock bird reserves, Sunderland's Winter Gardens and National Glass Centre and "Bede's World" at Jarrow.

Rivers of Industry

It was the lower reaches of the rivers Tyne and Wear that made this region one of the cradles of the Industrial Revolution. The mouth of the Wear (above) and the mouth of the Tyne (right) were the points of exit for the millions of tons of coal exported from the Northumberland and Durham Coalfield from as early as the 16th century and for the many ships built and launched along the two rivers. But long before that the river mouths had monasteries – Tynemouth Priory in the early 7th century and Monkwearmouth Monastery in 674.

Newcastle Upon Tyne Bridges

A succession of bridges, great feats of engineering and design, greet the eye along the Tyne quayside. In the photograph above the Millennium Bridge, downstream from the Gateshead Sage, is succeeded by the Tyne Bridge, the Swing Bridge and the High Level Bridge. The Tyne Bridge with its blue-painted iron superstructure (below), familiar to those television viewers who have watched the crowds of runners on the Great North Run swarming across it, carries the A167. It was built by the Middlesbrough engineers Dorman Long and opened by King George V in 1928. The Swing Bridge (next to the Tyne Bridge, below) was built in 1876 and was constructed so as to open to allow large ships to sail further upriver and to return downstream. Beyond the Swing Bridge lies the High Level Bridge, built by the great railway engineer Robert Stephenson to carry the main East Coast railway line between Edinburgh and London. The bridge was opened in 1850.

The "Blinking Bridge"

A dramatic addition to the riverside scene between Newcastle and Gateshead is the Millennium Bridge across the Tyne that was opened in 2001. The bridge, which is a spectacular feat of engineering, cost £22m. Like the Swing Bridge this, too, allows ships to proceed upstream, this time not by swinging open but by the pedestrian deck being raised towards the arch, hence its nickname the "Blinking Bridge". At night the arch is lit by powerful lights which change colour. And the lighting beneath the bridge forms beautiful reflections in the water. The bridge gives access to two important centres of art and culture on the south side of the river: the Sage Gateshead, a centre for music and the performing arts (right) and the Baltic Arts Centre, located in a converted grain warehouse and flour mill.

Newcastle Upon Tyne

Looking southwards across the city centre over the river Tyne towards Gateshead or looking up the river Tyne (above), one is struck by the fact that at one and the same time the river was an obstacle and at the same time a critical element in the city's growth. Although a Roman settlement was created here at an important bridging point, the city gained its name from the establishment of a Norman castle and its new name, in medieval Latin, recorded in 1168 was *Novum Castellum super Tinam*. Besides its castle the early town was surrounded by a stone wall and resisted several attacks from the Scots army in the 14th century. The export of coal from the surrounding coalfield from the Elizabethan period, and the related growth of shipbuilding and ship repair led to its long-lasting prosperity. Now these founding industries have disappeared and Newcastle, with a population of almost 190,000 is the regional capital of the North-East.

The Sage

Opened in 2004, the Sage Gateshead is a centre for musical performance. Located beside the Tyne on Gateshead Quayside, architecturally it is extraordinary, inside and out. The building, designed by Norman Foster and Partners, is constructed of stainless steel and covered by curving glass panels; it is particularly striking when seen from across the river. Opinion is divided on whether it is beautiful or ugly. It has been described sympathetically as a "resting armadillo" and as a "trilobite" fossil and derisively as a "slug". The centre contains a 1,700-seater auditorium, a 400-seater auditorium, a rehearsal room, a function room for conferences and even the concourse is acoustically designed for performances. It is the home of the Northern Sinfonia orchestra. It also has a local community function, containing not only cafes and bars, but also a music education centre and even a branch of Gateshead Public Library specialising in music and music education. Entry is free and the public is welcomed to watch rehearsals and music workshops.

The Castle and the Cathedral

Although vestiges of Newcastle's medieval street pattern still survive, all that remains of the medieval castle in Newcastle is the Castle Keep and the Black Gate. The original Norman castle dates from 1080 but of this nothing has survived. The keep (in the foreground on the left) dates from the reign of Henry II (1154-89) and the Black Gate across the railway from the reign of Henry III (1216-72). Beyond the Black Gate along St Nicholas Street stands St Nicholas, Newcastle's Anglican cathedral, which mainly dates from the 14th and 15th centuries. The tower surmounted by a spire, said to have been completed in 1448, reaches the prodigious height of 193ft (59m). Below is the view along Neville Street.

Northumbria University

Northumbria University came into being in 1992. Formerly Newcastle Polytechnic, this institution was in itself an amalgamation of Rutherford College of Technology, the College of Art and Industrial Design and the Municipal College of Commerce. In 1974 the City College of Education became part of the Polytechnic followed in 1976 by the Northern Counties College of Education. The university has two campuses, the City Campus and the Coach Lane Campus a few miles from the City Campus. The main campus is in two parts: Campus West and Campus East. Campus East (left and below) officially opened in July 2008. This futuristic-looking complex is the home of the School of Design, the School of Law and the Newcastle Business School. Campus East is part of a £136m investment by the university including a refurbishment of the original university city campus, Campus West. Among notable features of Campus East are rain harvesters on the roof for collecting water to flush toilets, solar panels to provide hot water, and building materials designed to let as much natural light as possible into the complex.

RAILWAY STATION

Newcastle Central Station, both the "train shed" and the forebuilding, was the work of John Dobson. It was officially opened by Queen Victoria in 1850 and is one of the finest railway stations in the country. Hard decisions had to be made about its location. Building it where it stands today meant that the castle keep would remain severed from the rest of the town as it had been since the railways had arrived between 1847-49, and a stretch of the town walls had to be demolished. If it had been built further north it would have destroyed the Holy Jesus Hospital and come very close to St Nicholas' parish church (now the cathedral). A location further north-west would have moved it away from the town centre.

EARL GREY'S MONUMENT

Dominating the townscape in Grainger Town, a part of central Newcastle designed and built in the 1830s and 1840s, is the monument to the 2nd Earl Grey (1764-1845) who was Prime Minister from 1830-34. While he was prime minister his government passed the parliamentary Reform Act, important factory legislation and the act abolishing slavery throughout the British Empire. The elegantly curved Grey Street, running away towards the top right-hand corner of the photograph, was recently voted by BBC Radio 4 listeners as the "Best Street in England". Prominent along Grey Street is the Theatre Royal which opened in 1835, with its fine classical portico. Grainger Town is also a special and stylish place in which to shop. It contains the triangular shaped Central Exchange Buildings, clearly visible in the photograph, built in 1837 with the Central Arcade cut through it from Grey Street to Market Street. The specialist shops sit below a barrel vaulted glass roof and sumptuous tiling. Close by is the Grainger Market, reckoned to be the largest indoor market in Europe when it opened in the 1830s. It contains a large number of greengrocers', butchers' and fishmongers' stalls and even has a unique Marks & Spencers "Penny Bazaar", the smallest Marks & Spencer store anywhere in the world.

Centre for Life

The Centre for Life, in Newcastle's city centre, west of the Central Station, is a science centre that aims to encourage a curiosity about science through a programme of events, hands-on exhibitions and debates about critical scientific and environmental issues that affect everyone's life. The centre is a registered charity. Among its attractions is The Dome, the North-East's biggest and newest planetarium. In The Dome images are projected onto a 360 degrees domed ceiling. Displays include a rocket launch, floating round the International Space Station and travelling through microscopic parts of the human body. An interesting approach to science education used by the centre is the deployment of "Science Explainers", young science graduates who interact with the public at exhibitions, run science shows and work with school groups. The Centre for Life has a well-developed science education programme that is used by more than 30,000 schoolchildren. The programme includes touring exhibitions and workshops for schools and adult groups are also accommodated. Outside the centre there is an ice rink in the winter.

St James' Park

St James' Park became the home of Newcastle United FC in 1892. The club was established as East End FC in 1881 and originally played at Chillingham Road in Heaton. The stadium has undergone great changes since its early days when facilities were very basic and the pitch had a pronounced slope. As early as 1905 the club won the League and lost in the Cup Final, drew very large crowds, and major improvements to the ground began quickly to take place. By the end of that year the ground had a capacity of 65,000. The record attendance of 68,386 was at a match in 1930 against Chelsea. Further ground improvements took place in the early 1970s with the construction of a 3,400-seater stand and in 1987 when the 6,607-seater Jackie Milburn stand was completed. The stadium was completely redeveloped in the 1990s in a £23.5m scheme under Sir John Hall's directorship that transformed St James' into a modern stadium with a capacity of just over 52,000. "The Magpies", so-called from their black and white striped shirts and black shorts, have had on their playing staff a succession of world-class attacking players including Jackie Milburn, George Robledo, Malcolm Macdonald, Peter Beardsley, Chris Waddle, Paul Gascoigne, Alan Shearer and Michael Owen.

Gateshead

Gateshead, Newcastle Upon Tyne's twin on the south bank of the river, like its more illustrious neighbour, flourished particularly in the 19th and early 20th centuries from its coal exports and its shipbuilding that have both now disappeared. Today its reputation lies in new industries such as the Komatsu earth digger plant (right) that employs 700 people and the MetroCentre, a vast shopping complex that attracts shoppers from across the region. In recent years Gateshead has also become known nationally and internationally through the development of a number of iconic cultural and artistic features and buildings. In 2001 the pedestrian Millennium Bridge across the river Tyne was opened, and nearby on the riverside are the Baltic Centre, a former flour mill turned into a contemporary arts centre and The Sage, a venue for music concerts. Beside the A1 stands the giant sculpture, The Angel of the North, greeting travellers to Gateshead. The Gateshead International Stadium (above and far right) has also gained an enviable reputation for staging regional, national and international athletics events. It also has outdoor pitches for soccer, rugby and hockey, and an indoor sports hall.

Gateshead International Stadium

Gateshead International Stadium began life as Gateshead Youth Stadium in 1955 opened by marathon runner Jim Peters. Later improvements have included the laying of a tartan synthetic track, a grandstand and floodlights. Brendan Foster broke the world 3,000 metres record here in 1974.

The stadium hosted the European Cup in Athletics in 1989 and 2000.

Angel of the North

The Angel of the North, by Antony Gormley, stands on a hill near the A1 and A167 roads and the East Coast Main Line railway line and announces to travellers from the south that they are arriving on Tyneside and to those travelling south that they are leaving it. Commissioned by Gateshead Council, the steel sculpture was erected in February 1998, having taken seven months to construct at Hartlepool Steel Fabrications Ltd. It stands 66ft (20m) tall, the wings have a span of 177ft (54m) and it weighs 165 tons (150 metric tonnes). Standing in an exposed position the foundations were especially carefully prepared to enable it to withstand very high winds. The sculpture is one of the most seen and commented on pieces of art in the world, for not only is the site visited by thousands of people but it is seen by millions of travellers every year.

Whitley Bay

Lying just 8 miles (13km) from Newcastle, Whitley Bay is a popular seaside resort and dormitory town for Newcastle Upon Tyne. Possessing a fine sandy beach, the town developed quickly as a local holiday destination after the opening of a railway link with Newcastle in 1882, a transport route still used by the Tyne and Wear Metro. One of the great attractions of Whitley Bay was its permanent fairground, The Spanish City, of which the centrepiece, the Dome, still exists.

St Mary's Lighthouse

St Mary's Lighthouse stands on a small rocky outcrop that is cut off from the mainland at high tide to the north of Whitley Bay in North Tyneside. It is no longer a working lighthouse (its light was decommissioned in 1984) but is open to visitors and has a small museum and visitors' centre. The monks from Tynemouth had a chapel here which at night would have had a lantern lit to warn ships to beware of the rocks.

Tynemouth

This small seaside community (left and above), blessed with both rocky shores and sandy beaches, lies at the mouth of the river Tyne, on its north bank in North Tyneside. The long stretch of beach known as Tynemouth Longsands has hosted the British National Surfing Championships. Overlooking the mouth of the river Tyne on the edge of the town is a statue of Admiral Collingwood, who was born in Newcastle and who gained fame as Nelson's second-in-command and the captain of the first ship, *Royal Sovereign*, to open fire in the Battle of Trafalgar in 1805. The town and its beaches attracted Victorian writers and artists as visitors including Charles Dodgson (Lewis Carroll), Dante Gabriel Rossetti and Charles Dickens. Every year the town (along with neighbouring North Shields) hosts the Fish Quay Festival, a festival of art, music and street celebrations that features a dramatic firework display. Since 2005 this festival has been joined by the Mouth of the Tyne Festival. Tynemouth is also at one end of the 140 miles (224km) long Sea-to-Sea cycle route which extends from the Cumbrian coast.

Tynemouth Priory and Castle

A Saxon priory was founded here in the early 7th century. It was attacked and plundered by Danish raiders in 800 and subsequently destroyed by further Danish raids. The ruins seen today (right) are the remains of a Benedictine Priory founded by monks from St Albans at the end of the 11th century. The castle ruins are the remains of stone medieval fortifications built after the prior of Tynemouth had been given royal permission to surround the monastery with stone walls. After the Dissolution of the Monasteries, the priory was dismantled except for the church and the prior's residence, but the castle remained in royal hands. Henry Percy, 9th Earl of Northumberland, who was implicated in the Gunpowder Plot was born in Tynemouth Castle in 1564. He was imprisoned in the Tower of London.

SOUTH SHIELDS

South Shields (above) lying between Tynemouth and Sunderland, has a population of 90,000. It is the site of a Roman fort, *Arbeia*, believed to be a supply port for Hadrian's Wall. During the Middle Ages the small temporary settlement called *Scheles* (temporary dwellings) developed into a permanent, small fishing port and by the 18th century this had been augmented by important glassmaking and salt-panning industries. In the 19th century its location beside the North Sea and with several miles of river frontage caused the town to grow rapidly. The growing demand for dyes and bleaches caused a massive growth in its alkali industry, the glass industry expanded, shipbuilding became established and coalmining and the export of coal became important industries. Now these mining and manufacturing industries have all but disappeared and many of the town's inhabitants commute to work in neighbouring Newcastle, Gateshead and Sunderland. But blessed with extensive beaches and a nearby rocky coastline, the town is a popular seaside resort.

Souter Lighthouse and Marsden Cliffs

Souter Lighthouse, located between South Shields and Sunderland, opened in 1871 and used the most up-to-date technology – alternating electric current. The lighthouse tower, engine room and the lighthouse-keeper's cottage are all open to the public. To the north and south of the lighthouse stretches an attractive coastline. To the south is Whitburn Coastal Park and to the north are Marsden Cliffs (left and above), almost vertical sea cliffs with wave-cut platforms at their base sometimes with detached sea stacks, including Marsden Rock (left). The cliffs have displays of primrose, sea thrift and common rock-rose and contain the most important colonies of seabirds between the Farne Isands in Northumberland and Bempton Cliffs in Yorkshire. Among species nesting are cormorants, fulmars, kittiwakes and herring gulls. In winter migrant species include snow bunting.

Sunderland

Sunderland stands at the mouth of the river Wear (above) on both banks of the river. At the mouth of the river and falling within its modern boundaries are the ancient settlements of Monkwearmouth (to the north) and Bishopwearmouth (to the south). Like its urban neighbours, Sunderland has passed through distinct phases of economic growth, decline and revival. Its function as a port, a centre for coalmining and the coal trade and shipbuilding began in the Middle Ages but expanded enormously during the 19th century and these industries, together with glassmaking, were the main employers until well into the 20th century. They have now all disappeared. Its role as a busy port in the 19th century made Sunderland the unwished for entry into England from the continent of a cholera epidemic on 19 October 1831. By early December more than 350 cases had been reported in Sunderland of which 119 proved fatal. By the time the epidemic had run its course through Great Britain and Ireland more than 56,000 people had died.

Rejuvenation

The last shipyard closed in 1988, the last glassworks in 2007 and the site of the last colliery is now occupied by a football ground. The chemical and electronics industries, paper-making and car manufacture have taken the place of these once staple industries. With economic decline and change, the riverside districts also went into decline but have been rejuvenated with the development of a marina, attractive apartments, the Riverside Retail Park and Sunderland FC's Stadium of Light (above). The single biggest employer in the Sunderland area is the Nissan car plant in Washington built on a 799-acre site. The plant with its neighbouring distribution centre (left) is the biggest car plant in the UK. Opened in 1986 the car plant employs 4,500 people.

Sunderland Centre

The panoramic view (left) over the centre of Sunderland from the south shows a number of the new developments that are transforming the city. In the far distance can be seen Roker and Seaburn beaches, which both have Blue Flag status. On the north bank of the river on the left is the Stadium of Light and on the right on the river's edge is the St Peter's campus of the University of Sunderland. Attached to this campus, housed in an innovative glass-roofed building, is the National Glass Centre Museum which opened in 1998. Beside the river Wear next to the Wearmouth Bridge is the stylish Echo 24 apartment building (left and above). Finally on Borough Road, in the foreground on the left and in close-up on the right, are Sunderland Museum and Winter Gardens. The museum tells the story of Sunderland's history and contains paintings by LS Lowry who was a frequent visitor to Seaburn. The Winter Gardens contain 1,500 plants in a rotunda of stainless steel and glass.

Stadium of Light

Sunderland FC's Stadium of Light, on the site of Monkwearmouth Colliery, opened its gates for the first time in 1997. The club was founded in 1879 and had previously played at six different grounds, the most famous of which was Roker Park where they played for 99 years. In 1933 more than 75,000 spectators attended a game at Roker Park against Derby County. When completed the Stadium of Light had three two-tier stands on the north, south and east sides and a Main Stand on the west side. After further expansion in 2001 the ground capacity was 48,300. Sunderland were FA Cup winners 3-1 in 1937 against Preston North End and again in 1973, when they were the underdogs, against Leeds United, winning 1-0.

Among the many great players who turned out for the club were English international Charlie Buchan who played between 1911 and 1925 and scored 209 goals, and the mesmeric Len Shackleton who played between 1948 and 1957 and was variously called the "Crown Prince" and the "Clown Prince" of British football.

Penshaw Monument

This monument (above) stands on Penshaw Hill at 444ft (136m) above sea level from which there are wonderful views. It was built in 1844 in honour of John George Lambton, 1st Earl of Durham. Lambton had a long political career and was Governor-General of Canada. Based on a Greek temple, the monument is 100ft (31m) long and 70ft (21m) high. Penshaw Hill is associated with the "Lambton Worm", a monster which according to folklore wound itself nine times around the hill. The story goes that the heir of the Lambton estates in the medieval period was fishing in the river Wear when he pulled out a worm. He tossed it down a well where it grew into a monster that he had to slay. Apparently the monster devoured the milk of nine cows every day and if not fed devoured man and beast.

Leechmere

This coastal suburb of Sunderland (left) lies to the south of the river Wear between Grangetown and Ryhope. Bordered by cliffs the coastline is within easy reach for the urban population and is a popular resort for families to walk and to picnic.

Washington

Washington (below and below left) expanded rapidly after 1964 when it was designated a New Town to take overspill populations from neighbouring towns and cities and now has a population of more than 60,000. But it is not all modern housing developments, new road systems and industrial estates. The town contains Washington Old Hall, a 17th century stone-built house which still contains some remains of the original medieval manor house inhabited by George Washington's ancestors. The Washington family took their name from their place of residence so that the capital city of the United States is named after this small town in Tyne and Wear. It is furnished with Jacobean furniture and there is a Jacobean garden that leads to the Nuttery, a nut orchard. Washington also has the 147-acre Washington Wetland Centre beside the river Wear. The centre has the largest heronry in the north-east of England and avocets breed there.

County Durham

County Durham is a county of great contrasts. Around and beyond the bustling urban concentrations, large and small, such as Darlington, Hartlepool, Peterlee and Consett there are some world-class visitor attractions. Parts of the county often missed by visitors are the Pennine areas in the west containing the very attractive upper Weardale. Then there are the interesting towns of Bishop Auckland, Barnard Castle and that gem, the cathedral city of Durham. There are the castles, such as Brancepeth, Lambton, Lumley and Raby and the smaller historical sites such as Egglestone Abbey and Finchale Priory. And, of course, there are two outstanding museums: Bowes set in its grand house and Beamish, the open-air museum that masterfully recreates life in the past in the north of England.

Castle, Cathedral and Priory

The panoramic view to the right shows the heart of the city of Durham bound inside a large meander of the river Wear. Caught within its wooded surround stand the cathedral, and the castle, now part of the university. Equally fascinating are the ruins of Finchale Priory that show in perfect detail the layout of a medieval monastic institution.

The Castle City

It is no coincidence that at Durham, on its easily defended site protected by a loop of the river Wear, that castle, cathedral and monastery were located together. The cathedral was the shrine of St Cuthbert and the medieval bishop was also a prince. By 1198 County Durham had been made into a "palatinate", a buffer state between England and Scotland, in which the ruling aristocrat had the powers of a king and had complete rule of the town's citizens and even minted his own coinage. And being a prince, and being in a buffer state he lived in a heavily defended castle. Outside the stone castle is Palace Green, the inner bailey of the castle, the cathedral and monastery occupying the outer bailey. The fortified citadel was connected to the rest of the town that grew up around it by two medieval bridges, Framwellgate Bridge (c1120), shown in the top right-hand corner of the photograph on the far left, and Elvet Bridge (1180). The castle is now occupied by the University of Durham, founded in 1833.

Durham Cathedral

The foundations of this beautiful Norman church (above and above right) were laid in 1089 by Bishop William of St Calais and the church was more or less complete when the porch ("galilee") at the western end of the church was completed in 1189. The western towers were added in the 13th century and the last medieval work was the top part of the crossing tower which is 218ft (76m) high, completed in 1487-88. On the south side of the nave are the cloisters of the Benedictine monastery that was once attached to the cathedral. Inside the cathedral, which contains the remains of St Cuthbert and the Venerable Bede, the nave is 201ft (62m) long with massive columns rising to the rib-vaulted ceiling.

Finchale Priory

The ruins of Finchale Priory (left and right) lie in a woodland setting beside the river Wear 4 miles (6km) from the city of Durham. Finchale was the site where the hermit Godric lived his life in poverty and isolation. He died after a long illness after being cared for by the monks of Durham who brought his remains to the small church at Finchale. In 1196 the Bishop of Durham endowed a priory at Finchale which only ever had a handful of monks living there, although it also functioned as a place of recuperation for the monks from Durham. The ruins, which show the priory layout in great detail, are Grade I listed and are in the care of English Heritage.

Brancepeth Castle

The romantic-looking Brancepeth Castle, 5 miles (8km) south-west of Durham, has everything that a castle should have: a gatehouse, a crenellated curtain wall and buttressed towers. The first castle on the site was a Norman castle but the present mighty edifice is largely a 19th century restoration carried out in the 1820s with further work completed later in the century. The most famous and notorious owners were the Neville family who had the castle removed from their ownership by the Crown because of their participation in the Rising of the North in 1569. In the early 18th century the castle was owned by Sir Henry Bellaysyse whose daughter became associated romantically with Bobby Shaftoe of popular song fame. The castle is still in private ownership.

Lanchester

As the panoramic view to the right shows, the village of Lanchester, 8 miles (13km) west of the city of Durham in the valley of the river Browney, is set in a very pretty agricultural landscape. The mosaic of fields surrounding the village, of various shapes and sizes with the field boundaries dotted with native broadleaved trees, is so typical of the English countryside. Its name, first recorded in a document in 1196, betrays its Roman origins, Lanchester meaning "long Ceaster", that is "long Roman fort". The Roman fort

Longovicium lay just to the south-west of the village. Burnhopeside Hall, near the village, was the residence of William Hedley (1779-1843), the locomotive engineer and designer who built the locomotives "Puffing Billy" and "Wylam Billy". "Puffing Billy", which first ran in 1813, is believed to be the oldest locomotive in the world and is on display in the Science Museum in London. "Wylam Billy" is in the Royal Museum in Edinburgh. There is a monument to William Hedley in All Saints parish church in Lanchester.

Chester-le-Street

The name Chester-le-Street means "the Roman fort on the Roman road". After the Viking raids on Lindisfarne in the late 8th century, St Cuthbert's remains were brought to Chester-le-Street before finally being removed to Durham in 995. The great attraction of the town today is a sports stadium. This is the Riverside Stadium of Durham County Cricket Club (above and left). Durham County Cricket Club was founded in 1882 but had a very long wait before becoming the newest first-class county team, elected in 1991. Durham were County Champions in 2008. Overlooked by the medieval Lumley Castle, the Riverside Stadium staged its first first-class county cricket match in May 1995 when Durham played Warwickshire. It became the newest Test match venue in 2003 when England played Zimbabwe. The ground has the distinction of being the most northerly Test match venue in the world!

Beamish

The award-winning Beamish Open Air Museum is a must for all families visiting the North-East. It is a wonderful portrayal of the social history of the region. Rural life can be investigated at the Home Farm and at the Colliery Village a clear picture can be gained of how coalminers and their families lived and worked nearly a century ago (including a visit to a drift mine). Then there is the Town (left) as it would have been in 1913, with among other attractions, a working pub and a railway station. And in complete contrast the Georgian Pockerley Manor House and its gardens can be visited. There are also tram and steam locomotive rides (above).

LUMLEY CASTLE

Lumley Castle (left and below) at Chester-le-Street overlooks Durham County Cricket Club's Riverside Stadium. The castle dates from the late 14th century with major alterations and additions by Sir Ralph Lumley who built the four massive, crenellated corner towers. It is now the property of the Earl of Scarbrough whose main home and estate is in South Yorkshire. The castle is now a luxury hotel and being near the Riverside Stadium it has been the hotel where visiting Test teams have stayed. It is said that several visiting Australian and West Indian Test players have been "spooked" by the ghost that is said to haunt the corridors and staircases of the castle. The ghost is said to be that of Lily, Lady Lumley, who was murdered by two Catholic priests because of her heretical views. It is said that her body was thrown down a well, which still survives, and from which she rises at night.

Lambton Castle

Lambton Castle lies between Washington and Chester-le-Street and belongs to the Lambton family, the Earls of Durham. Although at first sight it looks as if it were a medieval castle, it is in fact largely a creation of the early 19th century. It was built for John George Lambton, the 1st Earl of Durham (1792-1840), who was a successful politician. He was Lord Privy Seal and helped prepare the 1832 Reform Bill and then briefly was Governor General of Canada and wrote an influential report suggesting self government. The architects of the mock medieval castle were Joseph Bonomi and his son Ignatius, who were fashionable designers of country houses. The money for the re-design and building of Lambton Castle came from the profits of the collieries on Lambton land in the surrounding Durham Coalfield.

Seaham and Easington

Seaham and Easington lie close to each other at the coast. Seaham, the more northerly of the two, was previously called Seaham Harbour. Before industrialisation and urbanisation Seaham was a small village with a manor house and squire. The squire's daughter, Anne Isabella Milbanke, married the poet Lord Byron at Seaham Hall in 1815. After the estate was purchased by Lord Londonderry the place started to change. In 1828 the first harbour was built and trade increased once the first local colliery came into production in the 1840s. By the beginning of the 20th century the harbour was proving inadequate and a larger and more sophisticated harbour was opened in 1905. This is shown clearly in the photograph on the right. The last local coalmine was closed in the early 1990s. The Labour Prime Minister Ramsay MacDonald was Seaham's MP from 1929 to 1935 when he was defeated by the then renegade Independent Labour candidate, Emanuel (Manny) Shinwell who continued to represent the constituency until 1950. Easington (above) is made up of two settlements, Easington village and Easington Colliery. Easington suffered large levels of unemployment after the closure of its colliery in 1993.

Denemouth

Denemouth (right) is the seaward end of Castle Eden Dene, an important nature reserve. The Dene (an Anglo-Saxon word meaning a long curving valley) twists and turns on its way to the sea. The valley is heavily wooded but there are species-rich riverside glades. Native trees such as ash, yew, oak, wild cherry and bird cherry are all present and there are conifer plantings and a scattering of planted hornbeam and sweet and horse chestnut. The ground flora is very rich and includes bluebell, primrose and ramsons and the much less common herb paris, lily of the valley and giant bellflower.

Barnard Castle

Barnard Castle is not a castle but a town – but in the town there is a castle, Barnard Castle! The town lies just inside County Durham, beside the river Tees, where the river forms the boundary between Durham and Yorkshire. The old town is located on both sides of a long marketplace, alongside the castle, which is lined with shops and in which an outdoor market is still held (right). At the end of the marketplace are the grand Market Cross or Butter Market and the 12th century St Mary's parish church. The castle (above and below) dates from the very late 11th century but was reinforced and enlarged in the 12th century by the powerful Balliol family. Built on a river cliff high above the Tees, the castle occupied a superb defensive position. It was largely dismantled in the 17th century to provide building materials for the rebuilding of Raby Castle. But parts of the Great Hall and the 12th century cylindrical tower still survive. Charles Dickens visited the town, and stayed at the King's Head in the winter of 1837-38 when he was researching his novel *Nicholas Nickleby* which appeared in serial form in 1838-39. The reason for his stay was his surreptitious investigation of notorious boarding schools on which "Dotheboys Hall" and its headmaster Mr Wackford Squeers were based.

EGGLESTONE ABBEY

Located 1.5 miles downstream on the river Tees from Barnard Castle, Egglestone Abbey was founded between 1168 and 1198 by the Premonstratensian order. This order was founded by St Norbert in Prémontré, France in 1120. The Premonstratensians were known as the White Canons and were noted for founding their monastic houses in isolated locations, living in poverty and eating a frugal vegetarian diet. Egglestone was a poor abbey and its status as an abbey was threatened in the middle of the 13th century. It was also under constant threat of Scottish raids. By 1327 the monks had fled and the lands and goods of the abbey "destroyed, burned and wasted by frequent invasions of the Scots". After the Dissolution of the Monasteries in the 16th century part of the abbey was converted into a private residence but later largely demolished and some of the stone was used to pave a courtyard at a nearby country house. The ruins of the abbey church and the adjoining cloister survive. A recent field survey by English Heritage of the fields surrounding the abbey has revealed details of its water supply in the medieval period, the boundary of the monastic precinct and outlines of a garden that was laid out beside the private residence that was built there in the post-monastic period.

Bowes Museum

The Bowes Museum was created by John and Josephine Bowes. The building with its beautiful parterre gardens, in the style of a French chateau, opened its doors as a museum in 1892. There are galleries that tell the story of the couple and how and why they embarked on their brilliant museum project. There are eight other sets of galleries in the museum. The English Period rooms show English furniture and decorative art, there are ceramics galleries, a costume gallery and picture galleries exhibiting five centuries of pictorial art. Nor is local history and archaeology forgotten: there are two rooms telling the history of County Durham from prehistoric times to the present day. There is also accommodation for changing exhibitions. The most well-known exhibit in the museum is the automated Silver Swan which preens itself and catches a fish to the sound of music.

Raby Castle

Raby Castle lies in the Tees valley 8 miles (13km) to the north-east of Barnard Castle. It is one of the largest surviving medieval castles in the country and is set in a deer park surrounded by a high bank. Herds of red and fallow deer roam about the park. The estate belonged to King Canute in the early 11th century. Later it came into the possession of the Neville family who built the castle in the 14th century to replace an earlier fortified manor house. The Nevilles forfeited the property to the Crown because of their involvement in the Rising of the North in 1569, when northern aristocrats planned to replace Elizabeth on the throne by Mary Queen of Scots. Since 1626 it has been the property of Lord Barnard's family. The exterior is magnificent with a gatehouse and a series of crenellated towers. The interior contains a medieval kitchen that was used until 1954. There is also a series of magnificent gardens including an 18th century walled garden that had heated walls.

Bishop Auckland

Bishop Auckland is a market town and former coalmining town just over 10 miles (16km) south-west of the city of Durham. It owes the first part of its name to the fact that Auckland Castle, the palace of the Bishop of Durham, has been located there since the 12th century. Originally a hunting lodge, the castle stands in a former deer park that contains a magnificent deer house (above left) where the deer were fed in winter. The market town with its commodious marketplace (left) grew up along the route of an old Roman road next to the castle. The former railway viaduct over the Wear near the town was built in 1857 but the railway was closed in 1968. The viaduct was re-opened for road traffic in 1985 to relieve pressure on the medieval bridge in the valley below.

CONSETT

Consett lies 13 miles (21km) south-west of Newcastle Upon Tyne at an altitude of 850ft (260m) above sea level making it one of the highest towns in the country. It was formerly a heavy industrial town based on its steelworks. Despite its isolated inland location, the presence of coal, ironstone and limestone and a growing railway network to transport heavy goods made it a sound location for steelmaking in the 19th century. From being a small rural settlement Consett grew rapidly as workers and their families flocked there and it became a boom town. The steelworks closed in 1980 bringing large-scale unemployment. The town has now revived through the development of a range of light industries. Consett is famous for the Phileas Fogg Company, manufacturers of a range of snack-foods and Alan Godfrey Maps, publishers of old Ordnance Survey maps.

Teesside & North Yorkshire

This region is one of great contrasts, physical and human. It is dominated by Middlesbrough and the busy towns of Hartlepool, Billingham, Stockton-on-Tees and Darlington. Then there are the small seaside resorts of Redcar and Saltburn, the port and resort of Whitby, the coastal villages of Staithes and Robin Hood's Bay and the historic ruins of the once wealthy Whitby Abbey and Guisborough Priory. All this human endeavour has been made possible by making full use of the physical resources of the area, particularly the rivers and the coastal location. The rivers Tees and Esk are important gateways to the region and the resources at the coast: the beaches, the cliff scenery and the North Sea have all played a critical role in the cultural and economic development of the area.

Ports Large and Small

Two contrasting coastal scenes – the modern harbour of Teesport on the south bank of the river Tees with the industrial complex of chemical works on the north bank (above) and the huddle of red-roofed houses leading down to the tiny harbour at Robin Hood's Bay on Yorkshire's Heritage Coast (right).

Blackhall Rocks

Blackhall Rocks between Peterlee and Hartlepool is a nature reserve encompassing a grassed cliff top, limestone cliffs and the foreshore below. The cliff tops have a range of special plants including bird's-eye primrose, bloody crane's-bill and large winter-green. Grass-of-Parnassus flourishes in the wet places and orchids may also be found. Among butterflies found here are the common blue and a colony of the Northern brown argus (also known as the Castle Eden argus) that feeds on the common rock-rose. Seabirds and waders are regular visitors to the fore-shore. In winter migrants such as snow bunting and Arctic skua, on autumn passage from its breeding grounds in the high Arctic to its wintering quarters in the southern hemisphere, may also be spotted.

HARTLEPOOL

An early settlement was established close to Hartlepool Abbey, founded in 640. In the medieval period Hartlepool became a market town and the port of the Prince Bishops of Durham. It also became a small fishing port. Expansion of the town had to wait until the 19th century when it was connected with collieries to the west and became a leading coal-exporting port. A new settlement, West Hartlepool, grew up at this time to the south of the original settlement. Shipbuilding became important from the last quarter of the 19th century and the town was bombarded by the German fleet in 1914. Part of the docks have been converted into a marina. Below: the frigate HMS *Trincomalee*, Britain's oldest warship still afloat, in the dry dock at Hartlepool Historic Quay.

Middlesbrough

Middlesbrough, like Swindon in Wiltshire and Scunthorpe in Lincolnshire, was a Victorian new town. It had a population of only 154 in 1831, the year in which Joseph Pease of Darlington extended the pioneering Stockton to Darlington railway to Middlesbrough with the view of developing a port there to export coal from the southern part of the Durham Coalfield. By 1841 the population had grown to 5,000. Another big jump in the population took place after the discovery of iron ore in the nearby Cleveland Hills in 1850 and the setting up of ironworks. By 1861 the population had increased to 19,000. Towards the end of the 1860s the then Prime Minister, Gladstone, said the town was "the youngest child of England's enterprise, but, if an infant, an infant Hercules". The town continued to grow rapidly especially after steelmaking began in 1876 and by 1881 the population had risen to 56,000 and by 1901 to 91,000. The great names of Middlesbrough's iron and steel and engineering industries were Bolkow & Vaughan who set up works in 1841 and Dorman & Long, established in 1870. Iron and steel have now gone but the chemical industry thrives. In 2001 the population was 143,000.

The new town of Middlesbrough was laid out in a simple grid-pattern of streets around a central square which contained a marketplace and parish church. Despite much redevelopment in the second half of the 20th century, the grid-iron layout is still clearly visible and streets of identical terraced housing still survive (left and far left). The Civic Centre of the town (bottom left) has the Town Hall, County Court and Combined Court, the Middlesbrough Institute of Modern Art (MIMA) and the Central Library.

Above: the bus station in Newport Road. Left: the Town Hall fronting on to Victoria Square. The Town Hall, the grand flagship of the rapidly growing, confident town, was designed by GD Hoskins of Darlington and built between 1883 and 1889 in the Early English style at a cost of £130,000. At the Corporation Road end there is a tall tower and inside the great hall has a double hammerbeam roof made of iron.

CHEMICAL INDUSTRY

The chemical industry is the second largest manufacturing sector in the country and affects almost every aspect of our lives. And a significant share of that industry is concentrated in Teesside where it dominates large parts of the landscape as the photographs above and on the right show clearly. Distillation towers, catalytic converters and tank farms cover the riverside to the north and south of the river. Once there was only one employer (ICI) but today most of the world's largest chemical companies are represented on Teesside, including Amoco, BP, Dupont, Enron and Union Carbide. The industry employs 11,000 people directly and many thousands indirectly.

Bridges

Teesside is not only famous for building bridges but also for possessing two great examples of the bridge engineer's art. The Transporter Bridge, between Middlesbrough and Port Clarence, was opened in 1911 at a cost of £84,000. The distance between the two towers is 656ft (201m). A travelling compartment that can accommodate nine vehicles is suspended from the bridge and crosses the river in two and a half minutes. The Newport Bridge (below) was opened in 1934 by the Duke of York. The central part of the bridge between its two towers can be raised to allow large ships to pass through.

Riverside Stadium

Set right on the banks of the Tees is Middlesbrough FC's Riverside Stadium. The club was founded in 1876 and joined the Football League in 1899. The team played at a number of grounds until 1903 when the club moved to Ayresome Park where it remained for nearly a century, playing the last League game there in April 1995. The biggest gate at Ayresome Park was 53,396 against Newcastle in 1949. The ground was the venue for a number of matches in the 1966 World Cup. The new stadium, which cost £12m, has a seating capacity of just over 35,000.

Stockton-on-Tees

The name of Stockton-on-Tees will forever be associated with one major world event – the opening of the first steam passenger railway in 1825. The bill giving the go-ahead for the railway was passed by Parliament in 1821 and George Stephenson was appointed engineer. After the harvest in October he undertook a survey of the route helped by his son Robert. The first rails were laid on 13 May 1822 at St John's Crossing at Stockton. To cheering crowds all along the route the opening of the railway took place on 27 September 1825 when the steam locomotive *Locomotion* carried 600 passengers along the line.

Stockton-on-Tees

The town has a history stretching back long before the coming of the railway in 1825. The name Stockton, first recorded in 1196, has two possible meanings: either the "farm or village belonging to an individual called Stoc" or the "farmstead built of logs", most probably the former. It obtained a charter from the Bishop of Durham in 1310 to hold a weekly market and in 1376 a castle was mentioned in the records, but it was demolished in the 17th century and nothing now remains. Its heavy industries including chemicals, ship repair and engineering have all declined and its economy is now much more diversified. Among famous people associated with the town are Thomas Sheraton, furniture designer, born there in 1751, John Walker, inventor of the friction match in 1826, and Harold Macmillan who was the MP from 1924 to 1945 and Prime Minister from 1957 to 1963.

The riverside

Rejuvenation of the riverside areas of the town (left and far left) is a big priority and an ambitious long-term plan has been initiated. The town centre, which is reputed to have the widest main street in England (right) has also seen many new developments and Ropner Park has recently been refurbished thanks to a Heritage Lottery Fund grant. The photograph to the left shows a replica of Captain Cook's HMS *Endeavour* at anchor at Castlegate Quay. Between 1768 and 1771 Captain James Cook sailed in HMS *Endeavour* on a great voyage of discovery and charted the coasts of New Zealand and eastern Australia.

Darlington

Darlington (the name means the "farm of Deornoth's people") was founded on the banks of the river Skerne, a northern tributary of the Tees, and was first recorded in the middle of the 11th century. Being on the main north-south land route it developed as a market centre, Celia Fiennes in 1698 calling it "a great Market of all things". Renowned, like Stockton-on-Tees, for being associated with the world's first steam passenger railway line, opened in 1825, the locomotive that pulled the first train, *Locomotion*, still survives in Darlington Railway Museum.

The town was for more than a century an important locomotive building centre until the three works closed in the 1960s. The town centre with its tall clock tower over the Town Hall building and its covered and outdoor market (right) has been largely pedestrianised. Its railway station is still an important stop on the London to Edinburgh East Coast Line. The Quaker, Sir Joseph Pease (1799-1872) coal-owner, railway pioneer, co-founder of Middlesbrough and MP for South Durham, was born in Darlington.

Yarm

The odd sounding name, Yarm, is from an Old English word, meaning an "enclosure for catching fish" reflecting its riverside location (below) beside the river Tees and its tributary the river Leven. For centuries Yarm was the head of navigation of the river Tees. The attractive High Street is long, wide and very handsome. Even longer, and in some people's eyes, more handsome than the High Street, is the brick railway viaduct that runs parallel to it on the western edge of the town. This was built between 1849 and 1851 for the Leeds Northern Railway Company and has 43 arches.

REDCAR

With long sandy beaches and within easy reach of the rapidly growing industrial towns of Teesside it was inevitable that Redcar would become a popular seaside resort catering for the thousands of workers and their families cooped up for much of the year in polluted environments. The building of the Middlesbrough to Redcar railway in 1846 triggered its growth as a popular resort not only for Teesside but for people much further away in industrial West and South Yorkshire. Like most other resorts of its day, late Victorian Redcar had its seaside pier but this suffered from heavy damage over the years and it was finally demolished in 1981. Redcar is the home of the world's oldest lifeboat, the Zetland, that is housed in a seafront museum. One of the great attractions of the town is its independently-owned racecourse (right) which provides racing on 19 days during the year. Racing began in the area on the long sandy beaches before the race company set up its oval track in the town in 1875.

Skinningrove Cliffs

The beautiful cliffs (left) near Skinningrove, between Saltburn and Staithes are made of Lias shales and ironstone laid down in a tropical sea 190 million years ago and capped by boulder clay deposited at the end of the last Ice Age.

Saltburn-by-the-Sea

The cliff coastline, long sandy beaches and improved communications through railway construction caused Saltburn to grow into a small but fashionable Victorian seaside resort. An attractive feature of the resort is its 681ft (208m) long pier, though this is only half the length of the original pier that was completed in 1869 and restored in 1978. The pier is reached from the town by a cliff lift built in 1884, which replaced an earlier lift constructed in 1870.

Roseberry Topping

Roseberry Topping, located 6 miles (10km) south-east of Middlesbrough, rises to 1050ft (320m). A spur of the Cleveland Trail climbs up to the summit from which there are glorious views in every direction. The name was first recorded in 1119 as *Othenesberg* which means Odin's hill. The initial R is believed to have been added in error from the word "under" in the name of the neighbouring village of Newton-under-Roseberry. The assymetrical shape of the hill has been caused by the collapse of ironstone workings and because of its resulting similarity with the shape of the more famous mountain in Switzerland, has got the local nickname of the "Cleveland Matterhorn". It is now in the care of the National Trust.

Guisborough Priory

This Augustinian priory (left and right) was founded c1119. The priory was a wealthy house and held lands along the Yorkshire coast, in the Cleveland Plain running down to Teesside and in the North York Moors. Besides arable lands and important sheep and cattle ranches the priory also operated ironstone mines and was heavily involved in the salt-panning industry at Teesmouth and along the neighbouring Yorkshire coast. In 1289 a disastrous fire destroyed the original early 12th century priory church and work on a new church began almost immediately. It is part of this late 13th and 14th century church that forms the dramatic ruin that is the best-preserved part of the priory. It is the east end of the church with the shape of the nave and aisles well preserved. The outside wall has square buttresses, there are turrets above the nave and aisles and at the apex of the nave is a beautiful small window.

STAITHES

The dramatic setting of Staithes is almost without equal. Clustered around the harbour, the stone and white-painted cottages cling to the surrounding hillside hemmed in by high, almost vertical cliffs. The name comes from the old English "staeth" meaning a landing place. Staithes was once an important fishing port but the industry has now almost disappeared and the village has become a tourist attraction. It is said that Captain James Cook found his passion for the sea when as a youth he was apprenticed to a shopkeeper in the village. At the turn of the last century Staithes attracted a number of artists, who became known as the Staithes Group, and based themselves along the surrounding coastline and produced Impressionist-style paintings. The group included Dame Laura Knight and her husband Harold Knight who had a cottage in the village.

Hinderwell

The coastal village of Hinderwell is a remarkable example of a "street village" strung out along the A174 between Staithes and Runswick Bay, and surrounded by a rich agricultural landscape developed on the rich boulder clay soils of the area. The name is usually explained as meaning "Hilda's spring", Hilda being St Hilda, abbess of Whitby. As remarkable as its linear layout are the long medieval enclosures, usually called crofts, running back from the cottages on the village street, one of them now doubling as a caravan park.

Whitby

Whitby has so many historical associations: the site of a very early abbey, the whaling port, fishing port and popular seaside resort, and it has links with a number of outstanding literary figures including Mrs Gaskell, Lewis Carroll and Bram Stoker. Mrs Gaskell describes the whaling port of Whitby in her novel *Sylvia's Lovers* (1863) set in the Napoleonic period and Lewis Carroll is said to have thought of the idea of the Walrus and the Carpenter debating what to do with "such quantities of sand" in *Through the Looking-Glass* (1872) while walking on the sands between Whitby and Sandsend. Perhaps the most graphic use of Whitby in a novel was by Bram Stoker in his novel *Dracula* (1897). He had Count Dracula come ashore from a wrecked schooner in the guise of a large dog that scrambled up the 199 steps to the churchyard.

Whitby Harbour

The harbour at the mouth of the river Esk must have been a sight to behold when it was full of working ships. The only natural harbour of any size between the Humber and the Tees it was the base for ships that exported alum in the 17th and 18th centuries, for an important fleet of whalers in the 18th century and more recently for a herring fishing fleet.

Whitby Abbey

Whitby Abbey (left and above) was founded in 657 by St Hilda, abbess of Hartlepool. The first abbey was destroyed by the Vikings in 867. A second abbey was built in the late 11th century but the ruins that remain today are of a re-building of the 13th century. The architecture is interesting but it is the setting that bowls over the visitor. And the best way to visit it is on foot up the 199 steps from the town below before reaching St Mary's church and then going on to inspect the abbey ruins. St Mary's, set in its crowded churchyard, is basically medieval with Georgian improvements and replacements. The interior is full of galleries and box pews.

Whitby Lighthouse

For small and medium-sized ships plying the North Sea between Britain and the Continent and for the many colliers and other coastal vessels sailing between the North-East and London storms near the rocky coasts of Yorkshire were a constant hazard in the past and still remain so in the very worst of weather. For this reason lighthouses were important markers. Whitby Lighthouse was built in 1858 and automated in 1992. It stands on the cliff top at 270ft (73m) above the high water mark.

Robin Hood's Bay

Nikolaus Pevsner was of the opinion that Robin Hood's Bay is "without question the most picturesque fishing village of Yorkshire". Very few people would argue with that assertion. Perched above the sea wall beside the tiny harbour, from the beach it looks, and is, a real jumble of cottages, shops and other buildings large and small, mostly of stone, some painted white others not, and most roofed with red pantiles. An investigation of the streets and lanes in the village (which is better done coming down into Robin Hood's Bay rather

than going up the slope on which the town is built) reveals a network of narrow passages, some stepped and others coming to a dead end. The beach itself is also worth investigating in detail. At low tide the visitor can walk out into the bay stepping over a series of low broad steps of rock that curve round in the direction of Ravenscar to the south. And perched on the rocks are glacial "erratics" brought by the ice sheets in the Ice Age from Scotland or Scandinavia, dropped into the boulder clay when the ice melted and much later removed from the crumbling boulder clay cliffs by the battering of the waves.

Robin Hood's Bay

The name Robin Hood's Bay was first recorded in 1540 but there is no record of any association with Robin Hood although some authorities claim that he hid there. The proliferation of Robin Hood place-names up and down the country seems to have more to with the spread of the legend rather than the escapades of the outlaw himself. The locals refer to the old village as Bay Town. In the past the village is reputed to have been a centre for smuggling (almost all small isolated coastal communities seem to have such a reputation) and it is whispered that a network of underground passages link many of the old cottages in which brandy and tobacco were passed from supplier to customer. The novelist Leo Walmsley (1892-1966) was brought up in Robin Hood's Bay and used local settings of the village and surrounding coast and moorland in his *Bramblewick* series of novels written in the 1930s. The shore at Robin Hood's Bay lies at the eastern end of the Coast-to-Coast Walk which stretches from St Bee's Head in Cumbria across the Lake District, Yorkshire Dales and North York Moors National Parks to Robin Hood's Bay – a distance of 192 miles (307 km).